# ATHENS CITY SCHOOLS

SCHOOL_____ DATE OF PURCHASE 9/85

SUBJECT_____ GRADE_____

COMPANY PURCHASED FROM_____ B+

MORRISON ELEMENTARY SCHOOL
ROUTE 1, BOX 47
ATHENS, OHIO 45701-9708

# PLANET EARTH

# MOUNTAINS AND EARTH MOVEMENTS

## Iain Bain

The Bookwright Press
New York · 1984

# PLANET EARTH

**Coastlines**
**Volcanoes**
**The Oceans**
**Water on the Land**
**The Work of the Wind**
**Weather and Climate**
**Glaciers and Ice Sheets**
**Vegetation**
**Mountains and Earth Movements**
**The Solar System**

First published in the United States in 1984 by
The Bookwright Press,
387 Park Avenue South,
New York, NY10016

First published in 1984 by
Wayland (Publishers) Ltd
49 Lansdowne Place, Hove
East Sussex BN3 1HF, England

ISBN 0-531-03802-5
Library of Congress Catalog Card Number: 84-70746

Printed in Italy by
G. Canale & C.S.p.A. Turin

# Contents

# The Earth we live on

Have you ever heard the saying, "as old as the hills"? It is often used when we want to say that something is very old indeed. And it is difficult to imagine anything older than the great mountains that tower over many of the world's landscapes.

Almost all of them existed long before any human beings walked on the Earth. However, geologists (the scientists who study the Earth) now believe that many mountains, including the highest ranges, are among the Earth's youngest features. They believe that the Earth's surface is always changing and moving, and that the places where the highest mountains stand are where the change is most rapid.

This book is about the ways in which the Earth's surface moves and changes. You are probably wondering how such changes happen, or even how we know about them, since it is clear that we cannot often see the movement for ourselves. The

Opposite *The magnificent Himalayas, the world's highest mountain range.*

Above *The Earth has evolved over millions of years.*

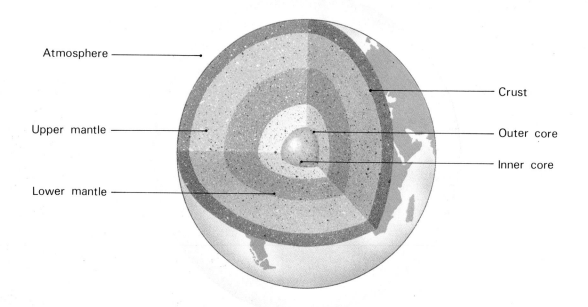

Atmosphere

Upper mantle

Lower mantle

Crust

Outer core

Inner core

*A cross section through the Earth.*

answer is that usually the change is very slow indeed, but it leaves behind signs of movement that scientists can interpret. Of course, sometimes the movement is fast enough for us to detect, when for example an **earthquake** occurs or a **volcano** erupts. We shall look at earthquakes and volcanoes a little later on in the book. First of all, let's take a closer look beneath the surface of the extraordinary planet on which we live.

## Inside our planet

One way of finding out what lies beneath our feet is to dig downward. Boreholes and mine shafts have allowed us to see what the Earth is like down to a depth of about 8 kilometers (5 miles). Down to that depth the Earth is made of rock. Rock is usually a very hard rigid substance, which makes it difficult to believe that the Earth is always on the move.

Rock is made up of crystals of various **minerals.** Some rocks are made up of pieces of other rocks. These are the

**sedimentary rocks** and they are formed from the particles of rock worn away by **erosion.** These particles were carried down toward seas, lakes or low-lying areas, where they gradually piled up, and over many years became squeezed into layers of solid rock. Other kinds of rock appear to have crystallized from what was once molten, or liquid, material.

Rock is not entirely rigid, though. An engineer would say that it has "elastic properties." That is not to say that rock is like a rubber ball, but it will bend, very slightly. And although it is strong, rock is likely to break if given a sudden sharp shock.

So, the Earth appears to have a rigid, rather brittle **crust.** Is it like that all the way down? Because no one has ever actually been to the center of the Earth to see what it is like, scientists have had to do a lot of detective work to find out.

First of all there is the difference in temperature and pressure. Early miners found that as they went down into mine shafts, it got hotter. This was one clue that led scientists to believe temperatures toward the center of the Earth could be very high. The clearest signal, though, came from erupting volcanoes that threw up fiery, liquid rock. As the molten rock cooled, it became hard and formed igneous rock. Finding igneous rock on the Earth's surface gave another clue to the scientists of the conditions deep inside.

The sheer weight of rock inside the Earth means that pressure, too, is very high. This gets higher toward the center.

Rock particles deposited on sea-bed

Layers of solid rock

*How sedimentary rock is formed.*

*Lava that has solidified, in mid-flow.*

Nowadays, scientists do not believe that the Earth is as hot as they once thought. But the center of the Earth is still pretty warm! The latest estimate is that temperatures in the center are about 4,300°C (7,800°F).

## The Earth's weight

In the nineteenth century, a man called J. H. Poynting invented a very ingenious balance that he used to weigh the Earth. He worked out its weight to be many millions of tons, and also proved that whatever the Earth is made of deep down is very heavy indeed. Scientists believe that the Earth's **core** is probably made up of iron and nickel.

Over the years, scientists have built up a picture of the Earth's interior. The hard, rigid outer part that we live on is the crust. This is from about 10 kilometers (6 miles) to 40 kilometers (25 miles) deep under the oceans, and about 70 kilometers (44 miles) deep under the continents or land masses. The continental crust stands up high, and has "roots" reaching deep down into the Earth. Below the crust is a layer called the **mantle.** This is made up mainly of igneous rock, and it reaches down 2,900 kilometers (1,800 miles) to the core. The core itself is divided into two parts; the outer part is liquid and the inner part is solid.

As far as movement is concerned, the part of the Earth that is most important is the upper part of the mantle. The crust is rigid, but the upper part of the mantle is not. Scientists think that perhaps as much as 10 percent of this region may be liquid rock. It is certainly the source of the molten rock that comes pouring out of volcanoes as **lava,** and cools to form masses of solidified igneous rock such as granite.

This zone, which reaches down to about 250 kilometers (155 miles), is called the **upper mantle.** No one is sure what it is actually like. It could be a sort of slush of solid crystals with liquid rock around them, or it might be like soft modeling clay. But whatever it is like in detail, it has one very important property, it can move. Very, very, slowly great currents are at work in the upper mantle, gradually moving material around as they carry heat from deep within the Earth up toward the surface.

*The smoking crater of a volcano.*

# Moving continents

Here is a game that you can play. Find an atlas with a map of the world. Trace the outlines of the continents and cut them out of your tracing paper. Now push the continents together and see if you can make them fit into one great island land mass. In some places the continents will fit together with difficulty, but in others, like South America and Africa, the fit will be surprisingly good.

What you have done on paper is what people have been doing in their imaginations ever since they had maps that accurately showed the proper shape of the continents. However, today it is more than a game. Scientists really do believe that the continents have moved.

The possibility that South America and Africa were once joined has been discussed for centuries. Toward the end of the last century, a geologist named Edward Suess suggested that once there had been a great southern continent, which he called Gondwanaland. This had broken up, he said, and the various parts had drifted away from each other to form the land masses we know today.

The idea of **continental drift** was taken further early this century, when a German scientist, called Alfred Wegener, showed that rocks and fossils in Africa and South America were very similar. He said that this was a sign that the two continents had once been joined. Very few people took him seriously, even though geologists and explorers were by then finding proof that the continents had once been closer together.

The problem was that nobody, not even Wegener, could work out how or why the continents moved. Today we know that the upper mantle below the crust is capable of moving, but in those days they believed it was quite rigid. If it was rigid how could the continents move? Also, Wegener believed that it was only the continental crust areas that moved. His idea was that the continents "drifted" through the oceanic crust. Since everyone believed that the crust beneath the oceans was also rigid, this made Wegener's theory very difficult to accept.

*The Earth from space, clearly showing Africa and South America, which may once have been joined.*

## One super-continent

Yet the evidence piled up to show that at one time the Earth's continents had been joined. Wegener's idea (like that of Edward Suess before him) was that about 200 million years ago, all the world's continents had been joined together in one super-continent, which he named Pangaea. Scientists studying the development, or evolution, of plants and animals discovered that many of them had evolved in the same way, up to the time when Wegener believed Pangaea had broken up. After that time they had started to evolve differently. There were also signs that, millions of years ago, parts of the world had climates very different from those they have now. The polar regions once had tropical climates, and in what are now hot places, such as Africa, India and Australia, there was snow and ice.

Soon after came the idea that currents flowed in the upper mantle, and that it was not entirely rigid after all. At last Wegener's ideas were accepted, although not until long after his death.

The final proof that the continents moved came from under the sea. Scientists had known for years that there

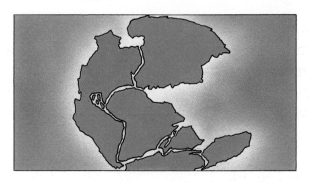

*The world as one super-continent.*

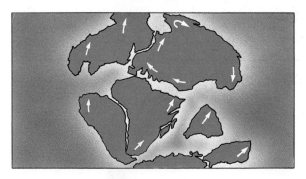

*The continents move apart.*

*The world map today. The continents are still moving.*

12

were great underwater mountain ranges in the middle of the world's oceans. In these **mid-ocean ridges** were active volcanoes, and scientists believed this was where material in the upper mantle burst through to form new crust.

When scientists dated the rocks that formed the seabed, they found that as they moved farther away from each side of the ridges the rocks got older. So it seemed that new crust was being formed on the ridges, and that new sea floor was spreading outward.

The idea of continental drift had now turned into the idea of **tectonic plate** movement. Today, scientists believe that the Earth's crust is divided up into about 12 tectonic plates, which include both oceanic crust and continental crust. Some of the plates are very large. For instance, Europe and Asia are part of one plate.

*The tectonic plates. The red dots are volcanoes and most lie along plate boundaries. The thin black boundary lines show where new crust is forming.*

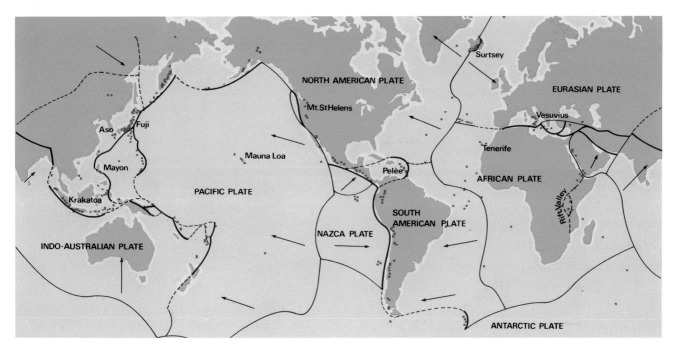

The plates are all moving slowly. They are mostly pulling apart at the mid-ocean ridges; in other places they are sliding past each other, and in some areas they are actually colliding.

The speeds at which they move have been calculated. The North Atlantic, for instance, is spreading at about 2 centimeters (1 inch) per year. India is crashing into Asia at more than 5 centimeters (2 inches) per year, in places. The fastest movement is in the southeast Pacific, where the Pacific plate and the Nazca plate are moving apart at more than 18 centimeters (7 inches) per year.

*A satellite view of Egypt, Suez and Saudi Arabia. The Red Sea is slowly widening, and the Arabian continent is gradually moving away from the African continent.*

# Mountain building

Mountains are immense. The Himalayas, Earth's highest mountain range, reach so far up into the Earth's **atmosphere** that most people who try to climb them need oxygen because the air is so thin at the top. Mountain ranges are usually great barriers that are difficult to cross. They certainly do shape our world, but what has shaped the mountains?

It is easy to see that mountainous areas have been formed by tremendous forces.

In the Canadian Rockies, geologists have found seashells thousands of meters above the present sealevel, and far away from the oceans where the shells originated. Parts of the European Alps, many kilometers from any sea, are made of limestone, a sedimentary rock that is formed on the seabed. In many places we can see how the rocks that make up the mountains have been folded and shaped by the forces that thrust them up into their present high-standing positions.

*Mount Everest, the world's highest peak.*

An early theory of mountain building was that when the Earth formed it was very hot and then it gradually cooled down. As it cooled and shrank the outer crust wrinkled and the "wrinkles" became the mountains. Nowadays scientists still believe that heat is involved, but in a different way. They think that mountain building has something to do with the currents that move about in the upper mantle, and is not something that happened at one particular time in the Earth's history.

This becomes clearer when we look at just where the world's mountains are. They are found in two great "belts," each made up of a number of mountain ranges. One belt runs from the Pyrenees in Western Europe, through the Alps, to the Caucasus in western Asia, and on to the mighty Himalayas and the mountains of China and eastern Siberia. The other belt runs from Alaska right down to the southern tip of South America. These belts occur where tectonic plates appear to be colliding.

Opposite *The Canadian Rockies began to form 60 to 70 million years ago.*

*The Sierra Nevada de Santa Marta, the northernmost section of the Andes.*

17

It is believed that when two plates move toward each other the part of the Earth's crust that is caught in between can be squeezed into about four-fifths of its original size. It is this squeezing that forces mountains upward.

The highest mountains occur where plates consisting of continental crust run into each other. It is happening at the moment as the Indo-Australian plate rams into Eurasia, forcing up the Himalayan mountains.

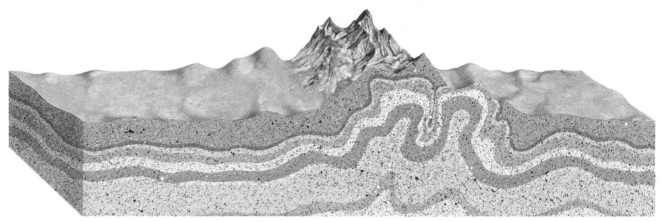

*The force of continental plates colliding pushes up mountains.*

*Mountains are also formed through subduction.*

Elsewhere, mountain building results from continental crust colliding with oceanic crust. What happens is that the continental crust rides up over the oceanic crust and forces it downward into the mantle. This process is called **subduction.** However, although material is moving downward into the mantle, the rumpling effect of the collision is enough to throw up great mountains. This is what has formed the Rockies and Andes mountains in the American continent.

## Undersea mountains

Tectonic plates also move apart where mantle currents move upward, and this creates mountains as well. If we drained the oceans we would see the mid-ocean ridges standing up from the ocean beds as huge mountain systems. They run down

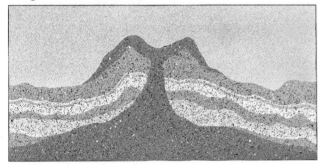

*Magma welling up to form new crust.*

the Atlantic Ocean, through the Indian Ocean and into the Pacific. The ridges are caused by hot, molten material, or **magma**, welling up into the gap left by the parting plates.

There are not many places where you can see this on dry land. Iceland is one place, but it is actually part of the Mid-Atlantic Ridge that peeps above the surface of the ocean. However in Africa you can see the continental crust pulling apart. The split occurs along the Great Rift Valley. The rift actually begins in the Middle East—the Jordan Valley is part of it, and the Red Sea, too. In Africa it cuts through Ethiopia and runs down to Malawi. The mid-ocean ridges have trenches running down their crests and the Great Rift Valley has exactly the same feature. On either side of it rise some of Africa's highest mountains.

Mountain building appears to have occurred at certain times in the Earth's history. About 60 to 70 million years ago, the Alps, Pyrenees, Himalayas, Rockies and Andes began to be pushed up. Although we are talking about millions of years ago, in geological history this is quite recent. In fact it is still going on and

the Himalayas are still slowly rising upward. About 250 million years ago there was another mountain-building phase that created the Caledonian mountains in Scotland and Scandinavia, the Appalachians in North America and the Massif Central in France. The Ural mountains of the USSR were also formed at this time. The Urals are quite low

*Opposite San Miguel Island in the Azores, part of the Mid-Atlantic Ridge.*

*The Massif Central, France, formed 250 million years ago.*

mountains, about 1,500 meters (5,000 feet), but they stand in the middle of a rigid plate marking an ancient collision.

There were other, earlier periods of mountain building—1,000 million, 1,800 million and 2,600 million years ago. However, the mountains that were thrown up then have long since vanished.

# Erosion and sinking

Many millions of years ago, the Cairngorm Mountains of Scotland were as tall as the Alps. Today they are only about 900 meters (3,000 feet) high. Just as there are powerful forces pushing up mountain masses, there are other forces causing them to shrink.

Erosion occurs on this planet because of its atmosphere and weather. Water gets into cracks in rocks and freezes. Pieces of rock are broken off high mountainsides and tumble down steep slopes. **Glaciers,** great rivers of ice, carry along fragments of rock that grind away at the ground over which the glacier flows. Running water in the form of rivers and streams wears away at the land surface. Sometimes rainwater actually dissolves rocks. Particles of stone and dissolved material are carried thousands of kilometers from the highest places on the Earth to the lowest.

Right and opposite *Millions of years of erosion have sculpted these canyons into fantastic shapes.*

We have seen how tectonic plates move *sideways* across the Earth's surface, carried by the currents that circle around in the upper mantle. There is another way in which the crust can move and that is *up and down*. This sort of movement is not the same as mountain building where the crust is rumpled up, or folded; it is a gentler sort of movement. Quite simply, it occurs when a tremendous weight is placed on the crust. When this happens the crust actually sinks down in the mantle.

How does this happen? One way in which the crust can be weighed down is by large amounts of **sediment.** All the material eroded from the higher areas on the Earth's surface eventually collects together in the lower parts, and usually into quite small areas. Much of the material eroded by rivers is deposited, or dumped, near the river's mouth, to form a delta. Lakes can also trap sediment, as can low-lying areas, or sedimentary "basins." As the sediments build up, the crust gradually sinks under the growing weight.

*Greenland is covered with glaciers.*

However it is not only the build-up of sediment that makes the crust sink. The sudden collection of a lot of water can have the same effect. Some years ago a large dam was built across the Zambezi River in southern Africa. Lake Kariba was formed behind the dam and grew to become one of the biggest lakes in Africa. But Lake Kariba had a surprise in store for the dam builders. The huge weight of the newly formed lake began to press into the ground underneath, and quite soon there were earthquakes near the lake as the crust sank.

## Glaciation

The most spectacular sinking has been caused by glaciation. In Antarctica and Greenland the ice is more than 3 kilometers (1.8 miles) thick. But under the ice caps there are places where the actual ground surface is lower than sea level. This is due to the weight of the ice pressing down on the crust. If you looked at a cross section of Greenland, you would see that this large island, with its high mountains around the sides, actually has the shape of a gigantic bowl.

You might wonder what would happen

if you took away the ice. The answer, of course, is that the ground would rise up again, and there are parts of the world where this has happened.

About 15,000 years ago, Scandinavia and most of the British Isles were covered by a huge ice sheet. It was probably 2 to 3 kilometers (1 to 2 miles) thick. It melted so suddenly that by 10,000 years ago there was little ice left. Freed of the weight of the ice, the ground began to rise up. This is called **isostatic rebound.** It has been worked out that part of Sweden has risen by 200 meters (656 feet) since then, and it is still rising by about 2 centimeters (1 inch) a year. Some scientists think that it will rise by another 200 meters (656 feet) before the rebound process is finally complete.

The British Isles are also rising, especially Scotland where there was most ice. You can see evidence of this rise at the coasts. When all the ice melted, the sea level rose rapidly and then gradually slowed. There were times when the rise in sea level exactly matched the rise of the land as it sprang slowly upward. When this happened, cliffs had time to develop, and you can see them today. Today, these shorelines are several meters higher than others, because the land is still rising while the sea level has not changed very much.

*Scottish cliffs, the result of isostatic rebound.*

# Faults and folds

The Earth's surface is always moving. But how does this movement happen and how does it affect material like rock? Earlier, we saw that rock is elastic; that is to say, it can bend a little. But you cannot bend a piece of rock very far before it cracks.

The movements the Earth's crust goes through tend to make it crack. Geologists call the cracks **faults.** There are faults all over the Earth's crust. Many of them happen at the edges of tectonic plates, where parts of the crust are colliding, or pulling apart. But there are plenty of faults elsewhere. Once the rocks in the crust have been broken they do not join up again very easily, and they will always be lines of weakness. A fault can be active (or moving) for a very long time indeed.

Faults may stay hidden deep within the Earth, but sometimes they can be seen. The piece of the crust which is Scotland has many large faults running through it. One of the most spectacular is the Highland Boundary Fault. It runs from near Stonehaven in the north east to Helensburgh in the west. When you pass over the fault line you cross from the sedimentary rocks of the Central Lowlands to the **metamorphic** and igneous rocks of the Highlands in a very short distance. Here, the rocks have moved along the fault, bringing very different rocks close together.

This type of fault is called a **transform fault,** which means that any movement that takes place is horizontal, or along the fault. But faults can also cause vertical, or up and down, movement.

Farther north, Scotland is crossed by the Great Glen Fault. It appears at the Earth's surface as a great valley containing a number of lakes, including Loch Ness. Movement along faults often weakens the rocks on either side, and the rocks around the Great Glen Fault have been eroded, or worn away, by glaciers. Geologists have been able to estimate how much movement there has been along the Great Glen Fault by matching up the rocks on either side of it. Normally, some of these rocks would be found nearly 100 kilometers (62 miles) apart. It is as if the northern and southern parts of Scotland were sliding past each other.

## San Andreas fault

A similar, but much more active fault is the San Andreas fault in California. Here, two tectonic plates are moving past each other, and the crust is tearing apart. The line of the fault is quite easily seen. You can actually see the effects of movement along the fault, where fences have been broken and roads pushed out of line. Over millions of years the total movement along the fault adds up to hundreds of miles.

Movement at faults can also be vertical. If you think of a fault as movement between two blocks of crust, then where

*Loch Lomond, part of the Highland Boundary Fault.*

the blocks touch is called the fault plane. The fault plane may be at an angle or be said to dip. **A normal fault** happens where the blocks are being pulled apart, and one side of the crust moves down the dipping fault plane. If the blocks are being squeezed together one side moves up the fault plane. This is called **thrust faulting.** Thrusting happens when tectonic plates are in full collision.

Faulting produces special kinds of scenery. Thrust faulting can push up

*The Vosges Mountains, France, are the result of thrust faulting.*

whole blocks of mountains. The Vosges Mountains in France are a good example of such a block mountain, or **horst.** Of course, when the ground slips down between two normal faults the opposite happens. It creates a valley called a **graben.**

A graben may occur where two plates

are pulling apart. The largest example of this is under the sea, where a rift valley has opened up on top of the mid-ocean ridges. On land the same thing can be seen in Africa's Great Rift Valley.

Rocks can bend without breaking. This is called folding. It happens when the crust is squeezed together by colliding plates. The folding is most intense at the point of collision. Farther away it becomes gentler and at last may die out.

*Africa's Great Rift Valley was formed when two plates pulled apart.*

Sometimes, very forceful thrusting pushes the folds up so far that they bend over each other.

During folding, rocks buried deep in the crust are under great pressure and heat. This can alter them completely. Rocks can become squeezed hard into banded **gneisses** or **schists.** The original rock layers can still be recognized in this new rock, although they have hardened and altered chemically. This changing process is called metamorphism, and the new rocks formed are known as metamorphic rocks. One of the most beautiful metamorphic rocks is marble, which is metamorphosed limestone.

*When two plates collide, rock is forced up and over into intense folds.*

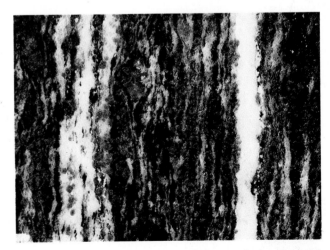

*An example of gneiss. The original rock layers are clearly visible.*

# Earthquakes

Have you ever been sitting in your house or classroom when a heavy truck is driving past? It makes a lot of noise and sometimes you can actually feel the rumble that it makes. Sometimes, passing traffic can cause the whole house to shake, and you can hear the windows rattling.

Now, just imagine that shaking getting stronger and stronger. Loose objects roll off shelves, dust comes down from the ceiling and cracks appear in plastered walls. This is what would happen if your house were being shaken by a small earthquake. If a large earthquake occurred you would probably want to get outside into the street or garden as fast as possible, because really large earthquakes can easily destroy buildings.

*The damage caused by an earthquake.*

In fact, earthquakes can create terrible damage and sometimes whole cities are brought crashing down. The amount of damage generally depends on the strength of the earthquake, but when buildings are flimsy an earthquake can cause chaos. In a bad earthquake in Khorasan, Iran, in 1968, many earth houses were destroyed, while those made of stronger material

*Here, the ground has literally been torn apart by an earthquake.*

survived. Most people killed in earthquakes die because their homes collapse on top of them.

The earthquake that cost most lives was probably the one at T'ang Shan in China in 1974. It is thought that over 500,000 people were killed.

Earthquakes tell us in a very direct way that the Earth can move. It is not always by the slow movement of tectonic plates or the gradual rise and fall of the Earth's crust. Earthquakes remind us that movement sometimes happens in sudden leaps and bounds.

But how does the steady, never-ending pressure of Earth movement become the sudden shock of an earthquake? As tectonic plates travel and collide with one another, they put a great strain on the rocks of the Earth's crust. As we have seen, rock is an "elastic" solid so it can bend a little to take that strain. But eventually the force may become too great, and the rock will snap suddenly, creating an earthquake. This is also the way in which a fault is formed. Once the fault is there, movement can go on happening along the fault line, in the form of earthquakes. The rocks on either side of a fault are very rough so there is a good deal of **friction** between them. Once again, for movement to take place, the strain must build up until it is greater than the force of friction. Sometimes this can take hundreds of years. Scientists are able to say *where* earthquakes are going to happen, with quite a lot of accuracy. But it is much more difficult for them to predict *when* one is likely to occur.

## Measuring earthquakes

Earthquakes have been studied for many years. As far back as AD 132 the Chinese had invented a simple device for measuring them.

This consisted of a heavy weight inside a bronze pot; when an earthquake happened the weight shook. The weight was connected by levers to eight bronze dragons' heads set around the outside of the pot. When the weight moved, a lever opened one dragon's mouth and released a little ball, which dropped down into the mouth of a bronze frog seated below! Besides showing that an earthquake had taken place, the device gave an idea of the direction from which the shock had come.

Today, scientists use an instrument called a **seismograph** to measure earthquakes. It can detect very small earthquakes, or those that are very far away, even on the other side of the Earth.

*Flooding caused by earthquake damage.*

Scientists have set up a network of seismographs all over the world. By working together and comparing results they can pinpoint the **focus** of an earthquake, which is the point down in the crust where the earthquake actually happens. They can also pinpoint the **epicenter,** which is the point on the surface directly above the focus.

Using seismographs, scientists have been able to learn a great deal about the Earth's interior. For instance, the seismographs show that earthquakes produce two main kinds of shock waves. One type is called a P-wave. This is a pressure wave. The other type is called an S-wave. This is a shear, or secondary, wave. The important difference between the two is that S-waves cannot pass through liquids. So when early seismologists picked up distant quakes and recorded only the P-waves, they decided that part of the Earth's interior must be liquid. Later on, evidence from seismic stations all over the world helped them to pinpoint regions such as the upper mantle and the outer core, which appeared to be liquid.

The chances of experiencing an earthquake depend very much on where you live. Most earthquakes happen in areas where tectonic plates are colliding. Some earthquakes occur on the ocean ridges, and a very small number, including the terrible one at T'ang Shan, happen deep down inside plates.

Every year there are actually around 800,000 earthquakes. But most of these are too small for people to notice. The really big ones that cause a lot of damage seem to occur at intervals of between 5 and 10 years.

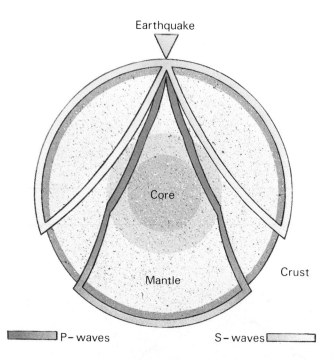

Earthquake

Core

Mantle

Crust

P- waves    S - waves

# Volcanoes

The upper mantle of the Earth is partly liquid. No one has ever been down to see for themselves, but we have sure and spectacular proof that molten rock exists deep below the Earth's surface—that is when it comes to the surface in a volcanic eruption.

Of course, you should remember that only a small part of the upper mantle is actually molten. For volcanoes to erupt there has to be a sort of stockpile, or reservoir, of molten rock to supply the

*A fiery lava flow pouring from a crack in the ground.*

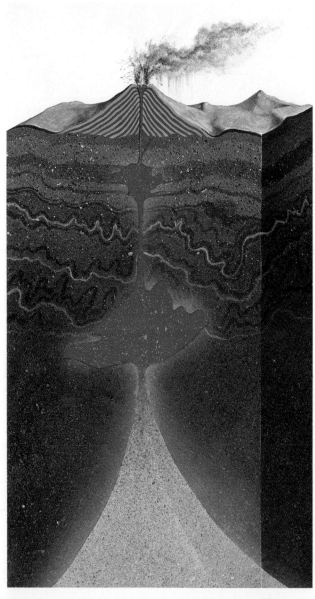

*Magma rises up from within the Earth.*

eruption. Molten rock is called magma and beneath each volcano, there is a reservoir, or **magma chamber.** Scientists know this because they have found the remains of old magma chambers, now "frozen" solid into masses of granite or **basalt** rock. Sometimes they can be seen on the Earth's surface as mountains, because they are not easily eroded.

How is a magma chamber created? Many of the Earth's volcanoes are found near the edges of tectonic plates, and this gives a clue. When plates collide one plate is very often forced down under the other. When this happens parts of the crust get buried deep in the mantle under the overriding plate. The rocks of the crust are often quite different from those in the mantle. They are lighter in weight and they may contain quite a lot of water. When they are drawn down into the hot mantle they tend to melt into pockets of magma and the pockets rise up again. If they get close enough to the surface, the molten magma may find a fault leading upward and so appear on the surface as erupting lava.

Opposite *A spectacular eruption.*

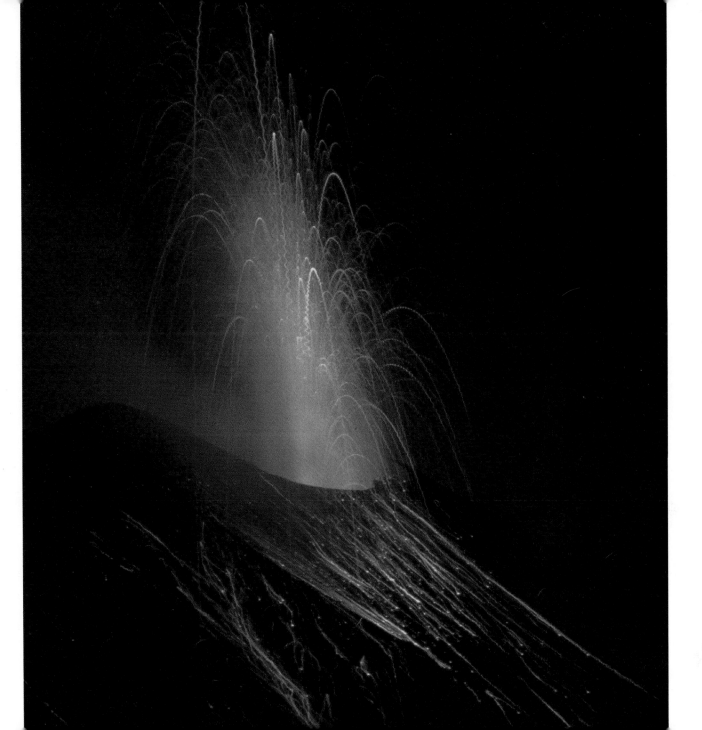

Many of the world's volcanoes are formed in this way, where a colliding plate is being forced downward. All the volcanoes on the west coast of the Americas, including Mount Saint Helens, were formed in this way. Volcanoes are also found where plates are pulling apart, and the magma wells up into the gap between them, forming new crust. Many undersea volcanoes are formed on the mid-ocean ridges in this way, and you can see this happening on Iceland, which is actually on the Mid-Atlantic Ridge.

## Extinct volcanoes

Away from the plate edges there are very few active volcanoes. However there are many extinct volcanoes. Often all that is left is remains of volcanic rock—the pipe of magma leading from the magma chamber to the surface. In Central Scotland, the castles of Edinburgh and Stirling are built on hills that are actually the remains of volcanic "necks". Almost whole volcanic **cones** can be found in France, in the Massif Central mountain

*A volcanic neck, known as Devil's Tower, in Wyoming.*

40

range, where erosion has not yet worn away the hardened ash and lava.

Volcanic eruptions can be very violent—it depends on how thick the lava is. If it is very thick, or viscous, it tends to solidify in the pipe of the volcano, forming a plug. Pressure builds up from underneath until it eventually blows out the plug in a great explosion. This is what happened at Mount Saint Helens in 1980.

One of the biggest volcanic eruptions ever happened in 1883, on the island of Krakatoa in the Indian Ocean. It made a bang that was heard 4,000 kilometers (2,500 miles) away, blew out ash and lava up to 80 kilometers (50 miles) high and caused a huge tidal wave that killed 36,000 people on nearby islands.

## Vesuvius

One of the most famous eruptions happened in Italy in AD 79. The volcano Vesuvius, which today overlooks the

*Mount Saint Helens erupted at 2 p.m. on May 18, 1980. The surrounding countryside was covered with ash and lava for miles around.*

modern city of Naples, erupted and buried the nearby town of Pompeii in volcanic ash. A lot of poisonous gas must have been thrown out too because many of Pompeii's citizens were suffocated, almost where they stood. After the eruption it rained heavily. This turned the ash into a kind of liquid cement, which, when it hardened, had the effect of preserving forever the shapes of the dead men, women, children and animals.

A volcano like Vesuvius erupts ash first, then lava. The thick lava does not flow very far before it hardens. After many eruptions the volcano tends to build

*A volcano at peace—San Pedro, Guatemala.*

*A volcanic eruption on Iceland.*

up a hardened cone around its opening. The cone is made up of different layers of ash and lava, which gives these volcanoes the name **strato-volcano,** after the Latin word *stratum,* meaning layer.

However, not all volcanoes are like this. If the lava is fairly thin then it may not solidify in the volcano's neck. Instead the volcano erupts fairly gently and almost all the time. Thinner lava flows more easily for longer distances, and sometimes forms a flat lava plain. This sort of volcano is called a **shield volcano,** and its **vent** or opening is often a fissure or crack in the ground. The best examples of shield volcanoes are found in Iceland and on the islands of Hawaii in the Pacific Ocean.

43

# Facts and figures

The highest mountain in the world is Mount Everest at 8,848 meters (29,000 feet).

The greatest mountain range on land is the Himalaya-Karakoram range. It contains 96 of the 109 mountains in the world higher than 7,300 meters (24,000 feet).

The greatest of all mountain ranges is under the sea. It is the Indian/East Pacific Ocean system, which extends from the Gulf of Aden to the Gulf of California. It is more than 30,700 kilometers (19,000 miles) in length. Its average height above the ocean bed is 2,430 meters (800 feet).

The greatest volcanic eruption ever recorded was that of the volcano Tambora, on the Indonesian island of Sumbawa, in 1815; 152 cubic kilometers (35 cubic miles) of material was ejected.

The most violent eruption ever recorded was that of Krakatoa in Indonesia, in 1883. The explosion was heard 4,000 kilometers (2,500 miles) away, and 18 cubic kilometers (4 cubic miles) of ash and lava were emitted. Scientists suspect that the biggest eruption ever was on the Greek island of Santorini in classical times.

The largest volcano is that of Mauna Kea on Hawaii. Its height, measured from the sea bed, is 10,000 meters (32,000 feet).

The highest active volcano is the Volcan Antofalla in Argentina, which is 6,500 meters (21,200 feet) high.

The deepest borehole in the world has been bored on the Kola Peninsula in the USSR. In November 1981, it had reached a depth of 11,000 meters (36,000 feet). The target depth is 15,000 meters (49,000 feet).

The deepest mine is the Western Deep Gold Mine at Carletonville, South Africa. Its depth is 3,800 meters (12,400 feet).

Perhaps the greatest earthquake in the world occurred in China in 1556, killing 830,000 people. In the 1974 earthquake at T'ang Shan, 500,000 people were killed.

The fastest movement between tectonic plates occurs where the Nazca and Pacific plates are separating in the eastern Pacific Ocean. The rate of separation has been estimated at 18.3 centimeters (7.1 inches) per year.

# Glossary

**Atmosphere**  The mixture of gases that surrounds the Earth. We call it air.

**Basalt**  A dark-colored, fine-grained igneous rock that forms a main part of the oceanic crust.

**Cone**  The hill of lava and ash that accumulates close to a volcanic vent.

**Continental drift**  The movement sideways of tectonic plates, which contain continental crust.

**Core**  The central part of the Earth, which is probably made of iron and nickel.

**Crater**  The depression formed around a volcanic vent, where material has been blown away by explosive eruptions.

**Crust**  The rigid, outermost part of the Earth.

**Earthquake**  The shaking effect produced by sudden movement along a fault line.

**Epicenter**  The point in the crust directly above an earthquake.

**Erosion**  The wearing away of the land surface, in particular by water—the sea, rivers, and rain.

**Fault**  A fracture in the Earth's crust.

**Focus**  The point deep in the crust where an earthquake happens.

**Glacier**  A large mass of ice that flows almost like a river, but at a very slow rate.

**Gneiss**  Layered, or banded, rock varying widely in chemical composition, see **metamorphic rock.**

**Graben**  Also called a rift valley, this is a valley formed where the land has sunk down between two parallel faults.

**Granite**  A coarse-grained, igneous rock that forms a main part of the continental crust.

**Horst**  A raised-up block of rock between two parallel faults.

**Igneous rock**  Rock that is formed when magma has cooled and solidified.

**Isostatic rebound**  Where the continental crust rises up again, freed from its weight of ice.

**Lava**  The molten rock erupted from a volcano.

**Magma**  The molten material that is found below the solid Earth's crust.

**Magma chamber**  The reservoir of magma beneath a volcano.

**Mantle**  The main section of the Earth's interior, between the core and the crust.

**Metamorphic rocks**  These are formed by the effects of heat and pressure, which change rocks physically and chemically.

**Mid-ocean ridge**  A rise on the ocean bed where plates are pulling apart and new crust is being formed.

**Minerals**  The natural substances with a definite chemical composition that occur in the Earth.

**Normal fault**  This happens when two blocks

of crust are pulling apart and one block slips downward.

**Sediment** Eroded material, such as sand, gravel and mud, that is deposited in seas, lakes and rivers.

**Sedimentary rocks** Rocks formed by eroded particles.

**Seismograph** An instrument that detects and measures earthquakes.

**Shield volcano** A volcano created by thin, free-flowing lava. It forms a very gently sloping cone.

**Strato-volcano** A volcano made of alternating layers of ash and lava.

**Subduction** The process by which an overriding tectonic plate forces a lower one down into the mantle.

**Tectonic plate** A rigid portion of the Earth's crust, which moves as a single unit.

**Thrust fault** Where two blocks of crust are being squeezed together, and one block is forced upward.

**Transform fault** A fault in the Earth's crust where movement is horizontal.

**Volcanic vent** The opening on the surface where magma appears.

**Volcano** A vent in the Earth's surface caused by magma forcing its way upward.

# Further reading

*Disastrous Volcanoes* by Melvin Berger (New York: Franklin Watts, 1981)

*Geology* by Dougal Dixon (New York: Franklin Watts, 1983)

*Earth in Motion* by R.V. Fodor (New York: Morrow, 1978)

*Disastrous Earthquakes* by Henry Gilfond (New York: Franklin Watts, 1981)

*Moving Continents* by Frederic Golden (New York: Scribner's, 1972)

*Volcanoes and Earthquakes* by Robert Irving (New York: Knopf, 1962)

*Earthquakes: New Scientific Theories About How and Why the Earth Shakes* by Patricia Lauber (New York: Random, 1972)

*Earthquakes: Our Restless Planet* by Margaret Reuter (Milwaukee, WI: Raintree, 1977)

*Earth Movers* by Mark Rich (Chicago: Children's Press, 1980)

# Index

# Picture Acknowledgments

The illustrations in this book were supplied by: John Cleare/Mountain Camera, *front cover,* 4, 16; Bruce Coleman Agency 8 (U. Hirsch), 9 (M. Freeman), 14 (NASA), 15 (D. & M. Plage), 17 (M. Freeman), 25 (N. Myers), 29 (E. Crichton), 40 (M. P. L. Fogden), 42 (M. Freeman), 43 (W. Ferchland); Bill Donohoe, artwork 6, 13, 18, 19, 36, 38; Geoscience Features Ltd. 5, 20, 21, 23, 30, 31 (below), 37, 39, 41; Photo Research International 11, 28, 33; Malcolm Walker, artwork 12; John Yates, artwork 7.